Paris Hilton

Paris Hilton is an American media personality, socialite, businesswoman, and DJ. She was born on February 17, 1981, in New York City, and is the great-granddaughter of Conrad Hilton, the founder of Hilton Hotels.

Paris Hilton gained significant media attention in the early 2000s as a socialite and reality television star, appearing on the show "The Simple Life" with her friend Nicole Richie. She also gained notoriety for her partying lifestyle, and her image was often associated with the "celebutante" culture of the time.

In addition to her reality TV work, Paris Hilton has also pursued a career in music, acting, and fashion. She has released several music albums and appeared in a number of films and TV shows. She has also launched a number of fashion and fragrance lines, and has been involved in various business ventures over the years.

Despite her controversial image in the past, Paris Hilton has also been involved in a number of philanthropic efforts over the years. She has supported a variety of charitable causes, including children's health, animal welfare, and LGBTQ+ rights.

Early life

Paris Hilton was born in New York City on February 17, 1981, to Richard Hilton and Kathy Hilton. Her father is a businessman and her mother is a socialite and former actress. Paris has three younger siblings: Nicky Hilton, Barron Hilton, and Conrad Hilton.

Paris was raised in luxury and attended private schools, including the Dwight School in New York City and the Canterbury School in Connecticut. She also spent time studying at the Provo Canyon School in Utah, a boarding school for troubled teens.

As a child, Paris was interested in modeling and acting. She began modeling at the age of 19 and signed with Donald Trump's modeling agency, T Management. She also made her acting debut in the film "Wishman" in 1993, when she was 12 years old.

Social scene and modeling (1996–2002)

In the late 1990s and early 2000s, Paris Hilton became a fixture on the New York City social scene. She was often photographed at parties and events, and her image was associated with the "it girl" culture of the time.

In 2000, Paris signed with the modeling agency Trump Model Management and began modeling for various brands and publications. She also made her runway debut at New York Fashion Week in 2000, walking for designers like Marc Bouwer and Catherine Malandrino.

Paris continued to make a name for herself in the fashion and entertainment industries, and in 2003, she and her friend Nicole Richie starred in the reality show "The Simple Life." The show followed the two socialites as they attempted to live and work on a farm in rural Arkansas. The show was a hit and ran for five seasons, from 2003 to 2007.

During this time, Paris also made headlines for her personal life, including her high-profile relationships with celebrities like Leonardo DiCaprio and Nick Carter. Her partying lifestyle and tabloid-worthy antics also drew attention from the media.

International stardom (2003–2007)

The reality show "The Simple Life" launched Paris Hilton to international stardom in the early 2000s. Her image as a glamorous, carefree socialite resonated with audiences around the world, and she became a household name.

Paris continued to capitalize on her fame, appearing in a number of films and TV shows, including "Zoolander," "The O.C.," and "Veronica Mars." She also released a self-titled album in 2006, which included the hit single "Stars Are Blind."

During this time, Paris became a prominent figure in the fashion and beauty industries. She launched her own line of fragrances, which became wildly popular, and also designed a line of handbags and accessories. In 2006, she was named "Best Dressed of the Year" by People magazine.

Paris's personal life continued to make headlines, and in 2006, she served a brief stint in jail for violating probation after a DUI arrest. The media scrutiny around her legal troubles and personal struggles intensified, and she took a step back from the public eye for a time.

Screen projects and endorsements (2008–2011)

After a brief hiatus, Paris Hilton continued to work in the entertainment industry in the late 2000s and early 2010s. She appeared in a number of films, including "Repo! The Genetic Opera," "The Hottie and the Nottie," and "House of Wax." She also made cameo appearances in TV shows like "My Name Is Earl" and "Supernatural."

In addition to her screen projects, Paris continued to endorse various products and brands. She served as a spokesperson for Carl's Jr. and starred in a number of their commercials. She also appeared in ads for companies like Guess, McDonald's, and Proactiv.

Paris continued to expand her business empire during this time, launching a line of hair extensions and a line of shoes. She also released a follow-up album, "Paris," in 2008, which featured collaborations with artists like Lil Wayne and Lady Gaga.

In 2009, Paris starred in another reality show, "Paris Hilton's My New BFF," in which contestants competed to become her new best friend. The show ran for two seasons.

Despite her continued success, Paris faced some personal challenges during this time, including a highly publicized breakup with her then-boyfriend Doug Reinhardt. She also dealt with the fallout from a sex tape that was leaked in 2003, which continued to be a source of controversy and speculation.

DJing, music and social media (2012–2019)

In the early 2010s, Paris Hilton began to focus more on her music career and became a popular DJ, performing at clubs and events around the world. She released several singles, including "Good Time" featuring Lil Wayne in 2013 and "I Need You" in 2018. She also collaborated with a number of other artists, including Afrojack and Dimitri Vegas & Like Mike.

Paris continued to work on various business ventures during this time, including a line of sunglasses and a line of clothing. She also launched her own fragrance line, which has become one of the most successful celebrity fragrance lines of all time.

In addition to her music and business pursuits, Paris also became known for her social media presence. She has millions of followers on platforms like Instagram and Twitter, where she shares glimpses into her life and promotes her various projects.

Paris's personal life continued to make headlines during this time, including her engagement to actor Chris Zylka in 2018, which was ultimately called off. She also spoke publicly about her experiences with abuse and trauma, and has become an advocate for mental health awareness.

In 2019, Paris released a documentary called "The American Meme," which explores the impact of social media on society and features interviews with other high-profile influencers and celebrities. The film received positive reviews and helped to solidify Paris's status as a cultural icon.

This Is Paris (2020–present)

In 2020, Paris Hilton released another documentary called "This Is Paris," which delves into her personal life and upbringing, as well as her experiences with trauma and abuse. The documentary received widespread acclaim and further cemented Paris's status as a cultural icon.

Since the release of the documentary, Paris has continued to be an advocate for mental health awareness, and has spoken publicly about her experiences with trauma and abuse. She has also used her platform to advocate for various causes, including animal rights and social justice.

In addition to her advocacy work, Paris has continued to work on various business ventures, including her fragrance line and her DJ career. She has also launched a line of skincare products and a line of CBD products.

Despite the challenges posed by the COVID-19 pandemic, Paris has remained active and engaged with her fans, often using social media to connect with her followers and share updates on her life and work. She remains one of the most recognizable and influential figures in popular culture.

Public image

Paris Hilton's public image has evolved over the course of her career. In the early 2000s, she was known primarily as a socialite and party girl, and was often portrayed in the media as vapid and superficial. However, as she has become more involved in business and advocacy work, her public image has become more complex and multifaceted.

In recent years, Paris has been recognized for her work as an advocate for mental health awareness and for her efforts to raise awareness about abuse and trauma. She has also been praised for her business acumen and her success as an entrepreneur, with her fragrance line and other ventures generating millions of dollars in revenue.

Despite her successes, Paris continues to be a controversial figure, with some critics arguing that her public persona is still rooted in superficiality and privilege. However, her fans admire her for her tenacity, creativity, and willingness to speak out about important issues.

Overall, Paris Hilton's public image is characterized by her ability to evolve and adapt to changing circumstances, and by her persistent efforts to use her platform for positive change.

Persona

Paris Hilton's public persona is often characterized by her glamorous, fashion-forward style, her bubbly personality, and her party girl image. She has often been portrayed as carefree, fun-loving, and unapologetically herself.

However, in recent years, Paris has also become known for her vulnerability and her willingness to speak openly about her personal struggles. She has spoken publicly about her experiences with abuse and trauma, and has become a powerful advocate for mental health awareness.

Despite the complexities of her public image, Paris remains one of the most recognizable and influential figures in popular culture. She has inspired countless fans with her entrepreneurial spirit, her dedication to social causes, and her unapologetic sense of self.

Catchphrases

Paris Hilton is known for several catchphrases that have become part of her public persona, including:

"That's hot." This phrase became one of Paris's signature expressions and was often used to describe something that she found fashionable or desirable.

"Loves it." This expression was frequently used by Paris to express enthusiasm or approval for something.

"That's huge." Paris often used this phrase to describe something that she found impressive or noteworthy.

"Screwed." This phrase was popularized by Paris on her reality show "The Simple Life" and was used to describe a situation that had gone wrong or become difficult.

These catchphrases have become a part of Paris Hilton's cultural legacy and have helped to shape her public image as a fun-loving, carefree personality with a unique sense of style and humor.

Media presence

Paris Hilton has been a ubiquitous presence in the media throughout her career. She has been the subject of countless articles, interviews, and news segments, and has been featured in numerous magazines, TV shows, and movies.

Paris first gained widespread media attention in the early 2000s as a result of her appearances on the reality show "The Simple Life," which followed her and fellow socialite Nicole Richie as they tried to live and work in rural America. The show was a massive success and helped to launch Paris's career as a media personality.

In the years since, Paris has continued to be a frequent presence in the media, with her fashion choices, personal life, and business ventures often making headlines. She has also used her platform to advocate for various causes, including animal rights and mental health awareness.

In recent years, Paris has become known for her social media presence, with millions of followers on platforms like Instagram and Twitter. She frequently shares glimpses into her life and work on these platforms, and has become a role model for aspiring influencers and entrepreneurs.

Overall, Paris Hilton's media presence is characterized by her ability to capture and maintain the public's attention, and by her willingness to use her platform to promote important causes and issues.

In popular culture

Paris Hilton has had a significant impact on popular culture, both in the United States and around the world. She has been the subject of countless songs, movies, TV shows, and other forms of media, and has inspired countless fashion trends and beauty products.

One of the most significant ways in which Paris has influenced popular culture is through her fashion sense. She is known for her distinctive style, which is characterized by bold prints, bright colors, and glamorous accessories. Her fashion choices have inspired countless trends over the years, and she has been credited with helping to popularize everything from trucker hats to chihuahuas as fashion accessories.

Paris has also had a significant impact on the world of music. She has been the subject of numerous songs, including "Stars Are Blind," which was a hit single in 2006. She has also worked as a DJ and has released several albums of her own.

In addition to her influence on fashion and music, Paris has also had a significant impact on reality TV and celebrity culture. Her appearances on shows like "The Simple Life" helped to popularize the reality TV genre, and she has been credited with helping to shape the way in which celebrities are portrayed in the media.

Overall, Paris Hilton's impact on popular culture is vast and multifaceted. She has helped to shape the way in which we think about fashion, beauty, music, and celebrity, and she continues to be a major cultural force to this day.

Cultural impact

Paris Hilton has had a significant cultural impact in a number of different areas. Some of the ways in which she has influenced popular culture include:

Fashion: Paris Hilton is known for her distinctive fashion sense, which has helped to shape popular fashion trends. She has been credited with popularizing everything from trucker hats to oversized sunglasses, and her fashion choices have had a major impact on the way in which we think about style.

Reality TV: Paris Hilton's appearances on reality TV shows like "The Simple Life" helped to popularize the reality TV genre and introduced a new kind of celebrity to the world. Her willingness to share her personal life on camera helped to shape the way in which we think about celebrity culture.

Beauty and Fragrances: Paris has launched a successful line of fragrances and beauty products, which have become popular worldwide. Her signature fragrances, in particular, have become bestsellers, and she has inspired countless other celebrities to launch their own beauty lines.

Social Media: Paris Hilton has been an early adopter of social media, and has been credited with helping to shape the way in which we think about influencer culture. Her millions of followers on platforms like Instagram and Twitter have made her one of the most influential people on social media.

Entrepreneurship: Paris Hilton is also known for her entrepreneurial spirit and has launched several successful businesses over the years, including a line of hotels, a fashion line, and a skincare line. Her success as an entrepreneur has inspired countless others to pursue their own business ventures.

Personal life

Paris Hilton's personal life has been the subject of much media attention over the years. Here are some key facts about her personal life:

Family: Paris Hilton was born into a wealthy family in New York City. Her great-grandfather, Conrad Hilton, founded the Hilton hotel chain, and her father, Richard Hilton, is a real estate developer.

Relationships: Paris has had several high-profile relationships over the years. She was previously engaged to model and businessman Jason Shaw, and has also been linked to actor Leonardo DiCaprio, Backstreet Boy Nick Carter, and socialite Stavros Niarchos III. She is currently engaged to entrepreneur Carter Reum.

Legal Issues: Paris has had several run-ins with the law over the years, including a 2007 conviction for driving under the influence. She has also been sued multiple times for breach of contract and other issues related to her businesses and personal life.

Philanthropy: Paris is an active philanthropist and has been involved with a number of charitable organizations over the years. She has been a longtime supporter of the Children's Hospital Los Angeles, and has also worked with organizations that support animal rights, disaster relief, and other important causes.

Health Issues: In 2020, Paris revealed that she has been diagnosed with PTSD (post-traumatic stress disorder) as a result of the emotional abuse she experienced while attending boarding school as a teenager. She has since become an advocate for mental health awareness and has used her platform to raise awareness of the issue.

Overall, Paris Hilton's personal life has been marked by both success and adversity. Despite the challenges she has faced, she has remained a positive and resilient figure, and continues to use her platform to make a positive impact on the world.

Relationships

Paris Hilton has had a number of high-profile relationships over the years. Here are some of her most notable romantic relationships:

Jason Shaw: Paris was engaged to model and businessman Jason Shaw from 2002 to 2003. The couple met in 2001 and were together for several months before getting engaged.

Nick Carter: Paris dated Backstreet Boys member Nick Carter for several months in 2003. The relationship was short-lived, but it generated a great deal of media attention at the time.

Stavros Niarchos III: Paris dated Greek shipping heir Stavros Niarchos III on and off from 2005 to 2007. The relationship was marked by a number of high-profile breakups and reconciliations.

Benji Madden: Paris dated Good Charlotte guitarist Benji Madden from 2008 to 2009. The couple's relationship was relatively low-key, but they were often photographed together at social events.

Doug Reinhardt: Paris dated former baseball player and reality TV star Doug Reinhardt on and off from 2009 to 2010. The relationship was featured prominently on the reality show "The World According to Paris."

Chris Zylka: Paris got engaged to actor Chris Zylka in early 2018, but the couple ended their engagement later that year. The breakup was relatively amicable, and the two have remained friends.

Carter Reum: Paris is currently engaged to entrepreneur Carter Reum. The couple got engaged in February 2021 and have been together since 2019.

Overall, Paris Hilton's romantic life has been the subject of much media attention over the years, but she has remained relatively private about her personal relationships. She has had a number of high-profile partners, but has also dated a number of people outside of the public eye.

Sex tape

In 2003, a sex tape featuring Paris Hilton and her then-boyfriend, Rick Salomon, was leaked to the public. The tape, which was filmed several years earlier, showed Hilton engaging in sexual activity with Salomon.

The release of the tape caused a media sensation, and it was widely circulated on the internet and in the tabloid press. Hilton initially denied that the tape existed, but later confirmed that it was authentic and that she had been humiliated by its release.

The sex tape had a significant impact on Paris Hilton's public image and career. While it initially generated a great deal of publicity for her, it also led to criticism and controversy, with many people questioning her values and reputation. Hilton has since expressed regret over the tape and has said that it was a painful experience for her.

Despite the controversy surrounding the sex tape, Paris Hilton has continued to have a successful career in entertainment, fashion, and other industries. While the tape was a significant setback for her at the time, she has shown resilience and perseverance in the years since its release.

Legal issues

Paris Hilton has had a number of legal issues over the years. Here are some of the most notable ones:

DUI arrests: In 2006, Paris Hilton was arrested for driving under the influence (DUI) in Los Angeles. She pleaded no contest and was sentenced to three years' probation. In 2007, she was pulled over and arrested again for driving with a suspended license, which violated the terms of her probation. She was sentenced to 45 days in jail, but was released after 23 days due to overcrowding in the facility.

Drug possession: In 2010, Paris Hilton was arrested in Las Vegas for cocaine possession. She pleaded guilty to two misdemeanor charges and was sentenced to one year of probation, 200 hours of community service, and a $2,000 fine.

Copyright infringement: In 2009, a federal judge ruled that Paris Hilton had violated copyright laws by using photos of herself taken by photographer Robert Rosen without his permission. She was ordered to pay $160,000 in damages.

Fraud allegations: In 2007, a lawsuit was filed against Paris Hilton alleging that she had failed to promote the 2006 movie "Pledge This!" as promised. The case was settled out of court for an undisclosed sum.

Breach of contract: In 2011, Paris Hilton was sued by Hairtech International for breach of contract. The company alleged that she had failed to fulfill her duties as a spokesperson for their hair extension products. The case was settled out of court for an undisclosed sum.

Overall, Paris Hilton's legal issues have been a source of controversy and negative publicity for her over the years. While some of the cases were relatively minor, others were more serious and had a significant impact on her career and public image. Despite these setbacks, however, Hilton has continued to maintain a high profile in entertainment, fashion, and other industries.

Bling Ring

The Bling Ring was a group of young people who burglarized the homes of several celebrities, including Paris Hilton, between 2008 and 2009. The group, which was made up of mostly teenagers from the Los Angeles area, stole millions of dollars' worth of designer clothes, jewelry, and other items from the homes of high-profile celebrities.

In the case of Paris Hilton, the Bling Ring broke into her Hollywood Hills home several times, stealing a number of expensive items, including jewelry, handbags, and clothing. The burglaries were eventually discovered, and several members of the group were arrested and charged with various crimes.

The Bling Ring case received a great deal of media attention, in part because of the high-profile nature of the victims and the audacity of the burglaries. Paris Hilton was one of the most prominent targets of the group, and her home was featured prominently in the 2013 film "The Bling Ring," which was based on the case.

While the Bling Ring was a criminal enterprise that caused significant harm to its victims, the case also highlighted the intense fascination that some young people have with celebrity culture and the desire for fame and wealth that it can inspire. Paris Hilton, who was one of the most prominent victims of the group, has spoken publicly about the experience and the impact it had on her life.

Printed in Great Britain
by Amazon

41826674R00030